BETTER BASEBALL
for Boys

BETTER BASEBALL
for Boys

George Sullivan

New and Completely Updated Edition

G.P. PUTNAM'S SONS · NEW YORK

PICTURE CREDITS

Aime LaMontagne, 16 (left), 22, 23 (upper right), 47. All
other photographs are by George Sullivan.

The author is grateful to the many individuals who
helped in the preparation of this book, particularly the
Wilshire Athletic Association of Springfield, Massa-
chusetts, and these officers of the association: Bernie
Gorman, former chairman of the Wilshire Board of
Directors; Jim Parzych, head coach, Wilshire Vikings;
and Steve Matroni, vice president, Wilshire AA. Special
thanks are also due these members of the Wilshire base-
ball teams who posed for the photographs that appear
in this book: Sean Batiste, Ricky Bennett, Daimon
Ciavola, Jim Conant, Joey Conant, Charlie Dippel,
Darrin Edwards, Sean Govoni, Michael Khouri, Timmy
Kotfila, Peter Racine, Billy Raleigh, Danny Scagliarini,
Joey Sciartelli, Scott Templeton, Craig Wisk, Chris
Wyler, Mark Wyler, and Joe Venditto.

The author is also grateful to Herb Field, Herb Field
Art Studio; Gary Wagner, Wagner International Photos;
Aime LaMontagne; and Bill Sullivan.

Library of Congress Cataloging-in-Publication Data
Sullivan, George, 1927-   Better baseball for boys.
1. Baseball—Juvenile literature. I. Title.
GV867.5.S93 1989 769.357—dc19 [E] 89-43111
CIP   AC   ISBN 0-399-61251-3
10 9 8 7 6 5 4

CONTENTS

BECOMING SKILLED

Everyone wants to play baseball, and play well. But not every player does, not at the beginning, anyway.

That's because many beginners don't understand the basic skills that are needed.

To take a small aluminum or wood bat and hit a small, white sphere traveling toward you at 60 or 70 miles an hour, and hit it within certain boundary lines, and do it so no one can catch it, is one of the most difficult things to do in the whole world of sport.

But the more you know about the art of hitting, the easier it becomes. A level, well-timed swing, without any dip or hitch, may not earn you a trip to the major leagues, but it will surely get you on base once or twice during a game.

The same applies to fielding a batted ball, to throwing, and running.

Once you know how to do these things the right way, the easier they become. And that's the purpose of this book—to show you the right way.

Another thing that's important is taking advantage of whatever natural gifts you have. Analyze yourself. Do you have good hands and a strong arm? Then think in terms of playing a position where fielding skills are vital. Shortstop, for instance.

Are you good at handling thrown balls and have some ability at the plate? Maybe first base is the position for you.

As in other aspects of the game, success in hitting comes from knowing what to do, then practicing.

Third basemen usually have good size, because they often have to use their bodies to block the ball. They're good hitters, too.

Outfielders have to have the speed to be able to go and get the ball and be adept at pulling down high flies and snaring line drives.

Some young players, no matter what position they play, display a certain inborn ability from the very beginning. They make the toughest fielding plays look easy. They hit the ball often and hard.

Even if you're not blessed with a great amount of natural ability, you can become skilled at hitting and fielding. All it takes is hard work. Once you know what's needed, then practice and practice. If there's any "secret" to success in baseball, that's it.

HOW TO HIT

To become a good hitter, you need a natural swing. That means your swing has to be suited to your size and build. There are 12- and 13-year-olds who are 6-feet tall and taller and can hit the ball a mile. That's fine; they can be sluggers.

But if you don't have the size and strength to be able to knock down fences, you should make up your mind to develop a good eye and become a "contact" hitter, a singles hitter. A hitter with a high average is more valuable to his team than the extra-base specialist. Successful hitting comes from taking advantage of what physical gifts you have and not trying to be something you can't be.

If you're like most young players, you'll want to copy the batting form of some major league player you watch on TV. This is usually a mistake. Your batting style has to be your own. Copying is very likely to do you more harm than good.

CHOOSING A BAT—Pick out a bat that feels comfortable. Should it be aluminum or wood? It doesn't make a great deal of difference. If you live where the weather gets chilly, you may find that a wood bat stings your hands on cold days. An aluminum bat won't. Also, if the ball should make contact with either the handle or very top of an aluminum bat, you might possibly get a base hit out of it. But when a pitched ball strikes the handle of a wood bat, it sometimes cracks it.

You should realize that a big, heavy bat won't

You can grip the bat at the end (above), or choke up.

make you a more powerful hitter. Bat control is what's important. Try bats of several different weights and lengths, and choose one that you can grip comfortably and swing easily. Be sure it's long enough to enable you to hit outside pitches.

GRIP AND STANCE—When you take your grip, you can either grasp the bat at the very end, your bottom hand flush against the knob, or you can choke up on the bat. When you choke up, the bottom hand grasps a few inches from the knob.

Sluggers almost always grip the bat at the end. A contact hitter chokes up.

Where you grip the bat can also be influenced by the timing of your swing. For example, if you have a tendency to swing late, then you should choke up. Choking up enables you to get the bat around faster. If you're swinging early at the pitches, grip the bat more toward the end.

You should also choke up anytime the pitcher gets two strikes on you. You'll thus increase your chances of making contact with the ball. In other words, it's less likely the pitcher will be able to pour over that third strike.

Be sure to grip the bat firmly. But beware of a grip that's too tight. You must keep your wrists and forearms relaxed in order to get a good swing. If you're tense, you won't be able to hit the ball past the pitcher.

Take your stance in about the middle of the batter's box. Keep close enough to the plate so you can reach any pitch over the outside corners.

Grip the bat firmly but not tightly; don't crouch.

Spread your feet about shoulder-width apart. Your back foot should point to the plate. Your front foot can point to the plate, too. But if it feels more comfortable, you can point the front foot more toward first base. This is known as opening the stance.

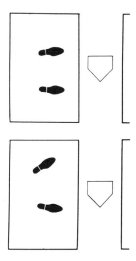

Recommended batting stances: square (top) and open.

Don't crouch. While you should bend your knees slightly, stand fairly straight. Keep your shoulders and hips level. Your weight should be evenly distributed on the balls of your feet.

As you await the pitch, cock the bat behind your shoulder. The bat end should be about letter high. Keep your elbows away from your body. Keep your head still.

Cock the bat behind your shoulder. Push off from your back foot and stride toward the pitcher with your front

THE SWING—Now the pitcher releases the ball. Cock the bat a little farther behind your shoulder, turning from the shoulders and hips. You're coiling up, getting ready to unleash your power.

To execute the swing, push off your back foot and stride toward the pitcher with your front foot. It doesn't have to be a long stride, only eight to ten inches.

Your arms swing the bat around with a quick snapping of the wrists. Keep watching the ball until it meets the bat. It should be a level swing; your hands should be letter high from start to finish. Meet the ball just in front of the plate, tightening your grip as you swing the bat through.

Be sure to follow through. After you've made contact, the wrists should continue to roll, the right wrist coming over the left.

It's a good idea to study your swing in a full-length mirror. The swing should be smooth and natural from beginning to end, with no lunging, no hitches, and it should always be a level swing. Young players sometimes develop the bad habit of uppercutting the ball.

"Bailing out" is a problem that some young hitters have. Bailing out stems from fear. When the ball comes whistling toward the plate, the batter has

10

foot. At the same time, whip the bat around. Be sure it's a level swing.

a natural tendency to want to get out of the way, to duck. He pulls one foot or the other away from the plate to avoid being hit.

You may be bailing out when a fast ball or curve comes in, and not even be aware of it. Have someone take a stick and draw a straight line through the batter's box that runs just behind both of your heels. Then have a fast-ball pitcher throw a few. After each pitch, check the positioning of your feet. If either heel is across the line, you're bailing out.

It's all right to bail out, of course, if the ball is actually coming toward *you*. But some young players get in the habit of pulling away from the plate on almost every pitch. This makes them easy victims for pitches that are low and outside.

What you must do, instead, is stride toward the pitcher as the pitch comes. Don't move your foot in any other direction. Make striding *toward the pitcher* a habit on every pitch, ball or strike.

When you're having trouble with a particular pitcher, you may want to alter your stance. If you're being fed curves, move several inches forward in the batter's box, that is, closer to the pitcher. You then may be able to make contact with the ball before it breaks. In the case of a fast-ball pitcher, move several inches deeper in the batter's box.

11

You can also help yourself by being aware of where the strike zone is located. In junior play, it's the area over home plate between your armpits and the top of your knees. Unless you have a clear idea of the strike zone, you're going to be swinging at bad pitches.

THE HIT AND RUN—The hit and run is one of baseball's most exciting plays. The runner on first base breaks for second on the pitch. The second baseman darts over to cover, hoping to prevent the steal. Thereupon, the batter punches the ball through

In junior play, the strike zone is the area over home plate between the armpits and the top of the knees.

the hole between first and second created when the second baseman vacated his position.

The situation above occurs when there's a right-handed batter at the plate. When a leftie is the batter, the infielder involved is the shortstop.

If you're the batter when the hit-and-run sign is flashed, hit the ball hard. Wait for the ball to come to you; concentrate. If it's outside, go and get it, punching it to the right side.

As the batter, you have the responsibility of swinging at the ball no matter where it's pitched, in or out of the strike zone. You've got to protect the runner.

THE SACRIFICE FLY—When there's a runner on third base and less than two out and you come to the plate, you may be instructed to hit a sacrifice fly. This is a fair or foul fly that is caught for an out, but must be long enough to permit the base runner to tag up and score. A sacrifice fly does not count as a time at bat, but you get credited with an RBI.

To hit a sacrifice fly, abandon your level swing and hit up a little, And be sure to swing hard. By swinging hard, you may not merely hit a long fly ball, you may even get a base hit.

A key factor is waiting for a pitch you can handle easily, the kind on which you normally hit a fly ball. This means that you can't let yourself get behind in the count. Once the pitcher gets two strikes on you, he's going to do all he can to make you strike out or ground out.

HOW TO BUNT

There are two kinds of bunts. There's the sacrifice bunt in which you're prepared to make an out so that a runner can advance to scoring position. There's also the bunt for a base hit.

Bunting may look easy, but it's not. There are major league players who have never become skilled in the art.

When you bunt, think in terms of "catching" the ball with the bat, not hitting it. Hold the bat almost as if it were a glove, and allow your hands to "give" a little when the ball arrives.

Getting the proper grip on the bat is vital. As the pitcher releases the ball, slide your top hand up the bat barrel to about the trademark, gripping lightly with your thumb on top and four fingers underneath. Your bottom hand remains where it was originally, down near the knob, with the knuckles facing the pitcher.

When executing a sacrifice bunt, step with your back foot and pivot on your front foot, so you end up facing the pitcher. Simply allow the bat to meet the ball.

A drag bunt. The bunter bunts and breaks for first base all in one motion.

At the same time you're getting your hands set, move your body into position. In the case of a sacrifice bunt, step with your back foot (your right foot, if you're a right-handed batter), pivoting on your front foot. You end up facing the pitcher. In other words, your bunting stance is something like a catcher's stance.

Hold the bat over the plate and level with the top of your strike zone, keeping it parallel with the ground. If the pitch comes in below the bat, bend in the waist and knees to allow the bat to meet it. Don't dip the bat.

Keep slightly crouched, your weight on the balls of your feet. Don't push the bat toward the ball. Simply allow the ball to meet the bat and rebound. Just as in catching a ball, your hands and arms should recoil slightly as the ball makes contact.

When you bunt for a base hit, it's different. Surprise is a key factor. If you give the other team advance warning of what you plan to do, the play isn't going to be successful.

Don't commit yourself until the pitcher has reached the point of no return in his delivery. Grasp the bat a little tighter than for a sacrifice and plan

RUNNING THE BASES

Successful base running depends more on speed than anything else. But by keeping alert, hustling, and knowing how to slide, you can make up for a limited amount of speed.

When you're at the plate and hit a ground ball, pop-up, or line drive, race to first base as fast as you can. Don't even think whether you're going to be safe or out. Just go! This also applies if the ball gets past the catcher on strike three or ball four.

Speedster Lou Brock of the St. Louis Cardinals, who holds the all-time major league base-stealing record, once said that he was capable of going down the line from the batter's box to first base in 3.4 or 3.5 seconds. As this suggests, getting a fast start is essential. If you're a right-handed batter, take your

When you race for first, use a sprinter's stride.

to meet the ball while on the move toward first base.

If you're a right-handed batter, dump the ball down the third base line or push it between the pitcher and first base, so that either the first baseman or second baseman will have to field it.

A left-handed batter usually tries to drag the ball down the first base line as he breaks for first base (hence, the term, "drag" bunt).

No matter where you intend to lay the ball down, step into the pitch as it comes. This helps to assure the bunt will be hit with authority and placed accurately.

15

Speed straight across the base. Turning slows you down.

first step with your rear foot, your right foot.

Use a sprinter's stride as you go, running on your toes, lifting your knees high, pumping your arms.

Lean forward slightly from the waist. Keep your chin up.

If it looms as a close play at first base, speed right across the base. But if it's a sure hit, veer to the right of the foul line after you've covered about half the distance to the base. This puts you in position to swing back and touch the inside edge of the base as you go by. Don't make the mistake of making too wide a turn when rounding first base.

Much of what's said above also applies to the other bases. Always touch the inside corner as you go by. And as you make contact, you should be heading in the direction of the next base. That's the

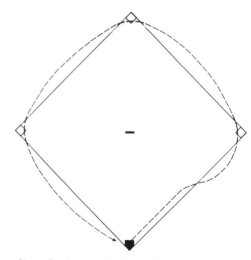

In rounding the bases, follow this route, touching the base corners in sequence as you fly by.

Left: When you take a lead, keep your weight evenly balanced on both feet, so you can move quickly to either the right or left.

Below: When you're a runner on third base, keep in foul territory. Then you can't be called out if hit by a batted ball.

most efficient way to run the bases.

Once you're a base runner and go to take a lead, keep your weight on the balls of your feet. Your knees should be bent, your body in a slight crouch. Let your hands hang loosely at your sides. You're ready to bolt to either your right or left. Keep your eyes glued on the pitcher.

If you take too big a lead and get trapped off base, a rundown is likely to result. Try to delay being tagged out for as long as possible. Make the defensive players keep throwing and throwing. The more throws they make, the greater the chance of error. At the same time, you're giving any other runners on base a chance to advance.

When tagging up on fly balls, crouch slightly, with one foot touching the base, the other foot well out in front and pointed in the direction you intend

to go. Listen for the coach's instructions. When he shouts out "Go!" tear for the next base or home plate. Even if it's a short fly and you have no intention of going to the next base, make enough of a feint to draw a throw.

When you're the runner on third base and you

take a lead, keep your feet in foul territory. (The foul line cuts the base path in half.) If you're in fair territory and get hit with a batted ball, you'll be called out.

You not only have to have certain well-defined skills to be a good base runner, you also have to be constantly aware of the game situation. Suppose you're the runner on second base. The batter lifts a fly into right field. Should you tag up, breaking for third base the moment the ball is caught?

It depends on the game situation. If your team needs a run, you'll undoubtedly be instructed to tag up. But if your team has a big lead, there's no need to risk advancing. It also depends on the outfielder who makes the catch, whether he's strong-armed or weak-armed.

Experience will help you to become a good base runner. Also learn to depend on the coaches. There are some situations when you have no other choice. Suppose you're on first base and a line drive is hit right down the first base line. You scoot to second and make the turn. Then what? Do you look over your shoulder to see what's happening? No. You look toward the third base coach. He'll signal you whether to keep going or not.

The same is true when you're the batter and slam the ball down the third base line. As you race toward the first base, you don't know whether the third baseman has made the play, or the ball has gone through into left field. Should you take a turn

In tag-up situations, watch the ball and listen to the coach.

at first or run at full throttle right over the base? Watch the first base coach. If there's a chance for two bases, he'll wave you on.

Always be aggressive on the bases, ready to capitalize on the smallest mistake. There will be times you can stretch a single into a double and a double into a triple. And by being daring, you can force the opposition to make mistakes.

Watch Pete Rose. He never fails to make a wide turn at first, forcing a hard throw from the outfield. He dives headfirst into the bases. When he's issued a base on balls, he *runs* to first base. Now, *that's* being aggressive.

SLIDING

On a close play, a good slide can spell the difference between being safe and being out.

There are three basic slides: the straight-on, the bent-leg, and the hook.

The straight-on slide is the simplest. Also called the feet-first slide, you can use it whenever you're trying to beat a throw. As you approach the base, you fall to one side, extending both legs, and sliding on one hip and your backside. Keep your arms off the ground.

The bent-leg slide is similar. Its purpose is to slow you down and permit you to get to your feet quickly so you can advance to the next base. As you near the base, fall to one side with both legs extended. As you begin to slide, bend one leg back, tucking it under the other. Keep your upper body erect.

Hit the bag with your front foot. To get up fast, simply push yourself up with the other leg, the bent leg. This, plus the momentum of the slide, will bring you to your feet quickly.

The hook slide is used more frequently than any other. It's called the hook slide because you slide past the base and "hook" it with one foot. Use the hook slide anytime you're trying to avoid being tagged.

In executing a hook slide, start the slide several inches to the right of the base as you're approaching

With the straight-on slide, you go into the base feet first, sliding on one hip.

The bent-leg slide enables you to get to your feet quickly so you can advance to the next base.

it. Slide on one hip and your backside. As you slide by, reach out with either your right or left foot and catch the base with your instep. You'll end up with your foot hooked to the base.

One other slide must be mentioned—the headfirst slide. In this, you go sliding into the base on your belly, your hands outstretched in front of you. This slide isn't recommended, except perhaps when you've been trapped off base and you're desperate to get back. Otherwise, the headfirst slide is too dangerous because you expose your face and hands to serious injury. If the man covering the base should decide to drop to one knee, you could even end up with a broken neck.

Practice sliding until you become skilled. When you practice, wear running shoes or sneakers, not cleats. The cleats can catch in the ground and cause an ankle sprain. Practice on the grass. It's a better surface on which to slide and it's easier on the hips and backside.

The hook slide. As he slides by, runner "hooks" the base with one foot.

STEALING

Speed. Timing. The ability to slide. These are the factors that make for successful base stealing.

It's a well-known fact that you steal off the pitcher, not the catcher. If you can get a big jump on the pitcher, then the catcher, even should he be armed with a cannon, won't be able to cut you down at second base.

In every stealing situation, the pitcher must, at some point in his windup, come to a full stop before pitching or throwing over to first base. If his next movement is toward the plate, the ball *must* go there, or he'll be charged with a balk. All the runners then move up a base. But before any such movement, he can throw to first.

As a prospective base stealer, it's up to you to detect clues in the pitcher's body movements that indicate when he's going to be sending the ball to the plate and when he's going to try to pick off the runner. You do this in the game's early stages, when you're watching from the bench.

Establish the pitcher's normal pitching motion in your mind's eye. Then determine what he does

Runner sprints for second after getting his jump on the pitcher.

The lead you take should be just big enough to enable you to turn, dive, and get back to the base safely on a pick-off attempt.

differently when he's going to throw to first. Study his head and shoulder movements and the way he adjusts his feet. In other words, play the role of a runner on first who is planning to steal, and look for what the runner would be looking for. Once you've spotted a flaw, a clue to what the pitcher's intentions are, you've won a big edge.

Once you're on base, getting a good lead is important. If you're of average size, you'll cover the distance between bases in fifteen strides. Take a 12-foot lead, and you'll cut two strides from that total.

But taking a long lead is risky. If it's *too* long, you'll become a pick-off victim. How long is too long? If you can't get back by turning and diving, and reaching with your hand as you hit the ground, you've strayed too far away. Establish the amount of distance you cover in your turn, dive, and reach. That's how much of a lead you should take.

When you take your lead, be sure your weight is

evenly balanced. You want to be able to go in either direction at the blink of an eye. And be sure you're on a direct line between first and second. Not being properly lined up can cost you a stride or two.

Some thieves stand motionless as the pitcher goes into his windup. Others bluff and bounce around. But all base stealers, no matter what their particular style, are able to *explode* away when the critical moment arrives. During practice sessions, be sure to work on developing your ability to accelerate quickly.

Getting a good lead, spotting some telltale movement in the pitcher's windup, then exploding toward second with bullet speed—all of these contribute toward getting a jump on the pitcher. Getting a good jump implies that you're going to be moving toward second before the ball leaves the pitcher's hand. When you get to second, you'll have to wait for the ball to arrive.

Every steal ends in a slide. As you rip toward second, watch the fielder's movements to determine where the ball will be coming in and, thus, how to slide. If it looks like there's going to be a close play, use a hook slide, going in on the right side of second base, hooking it with one foot.

But if it appears the throw is going to be late or off target, go straight in with a bent-leg slide. This enables you to get to your feet quickly in the event there's a chance to speed on to the next base.

An accomplished base stealer is a valuable player. A walk to him can be as good as a double, so pitchers can't afford to take chances with him. They must keep the ball in the strike zone.

Once he's on base, the opposition fielders can become rattled. The pitcher may get wild. Maury Wills of the Los Angeles Dodgers, one of base stealing's all-time greats, claimed that when he was on base it raised the average of a man at the plate by 20 to 30 percent. In baseball, obviously, crime pays.

PITCHING

Control. That's the one quality you *must* have as a pitcher.

You may be fast, you may be able to throw fast sharp-breaking pitches, but unless you can keep the ball in the strike zone, these skills won't count for very much.

The strike zone is the area between the batter's armpits and knees, across the width of the plate. Whenever you pitch, you should put the ball through the strike zone. But this shouldn't imply that you should aim the ball. Pitching is not like dart throwing. It's important to use your entire body to power the pitch toward the plate, not just your arm.

As you're developing a natural, rhythmic delivery, you should zip through the strike zone as a natural result of your stance, windup, and delivery.

THE WINDUP—If you watch much baseball, you know there are as many pitching styles as there are pitchers. As this may imply, you have to develop a windup that suits your particular size and build. Once you've developed a delivery that enables you to throw the ball with little effort and great effectiveness, stick with it. Use it on every pitch, whether you're delivering a fast ball, change-up, or curve. Only in that way can you prevent the batter from guessing what kind of pitch is coming. It's easier on the arm, too.

Most coaches advise young pitchers to use an overhand delivery, bringing the hand straight forward and down from above shoulder level. There's less strain on the arm with that type of delivery.

STANCE—Stand facing the catcher, the toe of your pivot foot, your right foot, over the edge of the pitching rubber. The left foot should be a few inches behind the rubber.

Keep fairly erect, your weight forward, as you peer in to take the sign from the catcher. Hold the ball behind your thigh, concealing it and your grip from the batter.

PUMP AND PIVOT—To get your body into the pitch, you pump. To pump is to swing the arms back and then forward. The pump is a rocking motion that helps to trigger the pivot.

As your arms swing up and over your head and your hands come together, the pivot begins. The right foot now points to the third base line, and your body has turned in that direction.

As your right arm goes back, kick your left foot up. Now you're looking at the batter over your left shoulder. Don't kick your left leg too high; you can throw yourself off-balance.

Just before you whip your pitching arm forward, stride straight ahead with your left foot. When you put it down, point it directly at the plate. Then swing your pitching arm forward and at the same time drive off the back foot.

Be sure to follow through. After the ball leaves your hand, keep your arm moving naturally. The

hand should reach a point outside your left knee. You'll be deeply bent at the waist.

In the final phase, the foot on which you pivoted, your right foot, comes to the ground slightly ahead of the left foot. You're in a squared-away stance in relation to the plate, your glove in front of your body. You're ready to dash in or move to the right or left to field the ball.

STRETCH POSITION—When there are runners on base, you have to give up your usual delivery in

Pitcher gets sign from the catcher, then pumps, pivots on the right foot, kicks the left foot high in the air as he strides forward and whips the ball in.

favor of a stretch. Were you to use your full windup, the amount of time involved would give the base runners a good chance of stealing. But when you use the stretch, the runners must keep close to their bases.

In taking a stretch, stand sideways to the plate,

27

In pitching from a stretch position, stand sideways to the plate. You can't use a big kick. From start to finish, it's an abbreviated delivery.

facing third base. Place your right foot on the rubber. Your left foot should be angled slightly toward the plate.

Hold your hands together about chest high. Your pitching hand should be gripping the ball in your glove. Turn your head in the direction of first base, and watch the runner out of the corner of your eye. You can turn your head to glance at the catcher and then look back toward the runner, and you can keep doing this, but your hands must come to a complete stop before you go into your windup.

In delivering the ball, quickly shift your weight back and then forward, pushing off from your right foot, striding forward with your left foot. Don't lift your left leg as high as in your normal delivery. The runners can take advantage of a big kick. Keep your foot close to the ground when you step.

It's important to remember that once you put your right foot in contact with the rubber, your delivery enters a critical phase. After that, whenever you make a move toward either first base or the plate, you must throw the ball there. Otherwise, a balk will be called.

You are, however, permitted to fake a throw to either second base or third base. A balk can also be called for failing to come to a set position before delivering the ball.

GRIPS—You don't have to be fancy to be an effective pitcher, as the opening paragraphs of this section point out. You don't have to have many

Fast ball grip

pitches in your repertoire. You don't need any trick or freak pitches. Not only are they not needed, you can injure your arm by tinkering with them.

All you need is a fast ball and a change of pace—and the skill to control them. If you're 12 or 13 or so, you may also want to develop a curve ball. But it's no necessity.

To throw a fast ball, grip the ball with the index

The change-up

Curve-ball grip

and middle fingers just along the seams. The thumb grips from beneath.

When you deliver, the ball rolls off the ends of the gripping fingers. This imparts backspin to the ball, causing it to rise slightly, or "tail" up.

The change-up is a slow pitch thrown for deception. But in order to deceive, it must be thrown with the same motion as the fast ball. In other words, the batter swings at your motion, not at the pitch itself.

To deliver the change-up, nestle the ball well back in your hand. Use a full finger grip. Keep your wrist locked as you release.

For a curve, grip the ball with the first two fingers across the seams. The thumb is underneath.

When you deliver, the wrist turns to the right and the ball snaps off the index finger. This causes the ball to spin from left to right, and it breaks in the same direction.

It isn't the size of the curve that's important. It's where you put it. You have to keep the ball low in the strike zone for the curve to be an effective pitch.

It takes plenty of practice to master the curve and other such pitches. If you become consistently effective with the pitch inside of three years, you're doing well.

30

CATCHING

The position of catcher is probably the toughest of all. The man behind the plate has to have a sturdy body, strong legs, and a good throwing arm. The job takes stamina, too, for you have to be able to spend long periods of time in a squatting position while wearing all that equipment. On a hot day, that's no picnic.

The position is demanding in other ways. As the only player on the field who is facing all the players, the catcher can see and assess every game situation. Thus, the catcher is a field general, directing cutoffs and relays, infield throws, and other fielding plays, such as those that occur on bunt attempts. All this, and the catcher also has to handle the pitcher.

STANCE—As the catcher, you operate out of a squat position, your feet comfortably apart. Your

Giving the sign; use your right knee and glove to block the coaches' view.

Catcher wears protective headgear.

weight should be concentrated on the balls of your feet. Keep your knees wide apart.

As you give the sign, point your right knee toward the pitcher. The knee conceals the sign from the first base coach. Put your mitt in front of your left knee to hide the sign from the third base coach.

In actually giving the sign, hold the fingers of the right hand inside the right thigh. Since the opposition can't see them, the signs don't have to be complicated. One finger can represent a fast ball, two fingers a change-up, etc.

Presenting the target; notice how the catcher has shifted his weight.

Get down low to block low pitches.

After you've given the sign, spread your feet and rise up somewhat. Keep your left foot slightly ahead of the right. Get as close to the batter as you can.

Now give the pitcher a target with your mitt, holding it about chin high. Keep your throwing hand relaxed, the fingers closed.

CATCHING THE BALL—Catch every ball in the strike zone (the area above the plate between the batter's armpits and his knees) with the fingers up.

On steal attempts, rise up, take a stride, and fire toward the base.

Let your hands "give" with the pitch. Bring the ball to your belt buckle. Low pitches, even low strikes, should be caught with the fingers down.

Try to catch every ball in the middle of your body. This means you'll have to shift your feet on some pitches. But shift them only when the pitch is well outside the strike zone. Otherwise, you might influence the umpire to call a strike a ball.

Get your legs down on the ground to block low pitches, unless a man is attempting to steal. In that

Get down on one or both knees to block a runner rampaging in from third base.

case, try to scoop up the ball like an infielder.

THROWING—While it's important that you, as the catcher, be strong-armed, it's even more important that you be accurate and able to get the ball away quickly. It takes practice to develop these qualities. As soon as you see the runner going and you have the ball in your possession, spring to your feet, stride forward on your left foot, and gun the ball to second base.

Throw overhand. If you don't, the ball will curve or hook and is likely to be off-target as a result.

Deliver the ball to about knee level of the man who is to receive it. Don't wait for the man to get to the base. Just throw. It's his responsibility to be there when the ball arrives.

CATCHING POP-UPS—A right-handed batter will almost always foul an outside pitch to your right and an inside pitch to your left. The opposite holds true in the case of a left-handed batter. He'll foul an outside pitch to your left and inside pitch to your right. Keep this in mind when running for a foul pop-up.

As the ball shoots toward the sky, slide your mask over your head and hold it for a split second until you've located the ball. Then toss the mask in the opposite direction. This prevents you from tripping on it.

Get to the spot where the ball is going to drop. Stand directly under it as it descends, then take a step back and make the catch. Simply hold the glove

34

flat in front of your chest and let the ball drop into it. But be sure to watch the ball all the way.

Bear in mind that a pop fly behind the plate will tend to drift toward the infield because of the way in which it's rotating. Be sure to allow for this drift.

COVERING THE PLATE—When a runner comes barreling in from third base, drop to one knee or both knees, hold the ball in your bare hand, covering it with your glove, and try to tag the runner with the back side of the mitt. Be wary of the bare-handed tag. It can result in an injury.

Remember, the catcher isn't permitted to stand in the base line, blocking the runner's path to the plate, unless he has the ball in his possession or is about to catch a throw.

Forced plays at home are easier. All you have to do is step on the plate, making the play like a first baseman. On double play attempts, make your throw to first base on the inside of the base line to avoid hitting the runner.

FIELDING GROUNDERS—The ground balls the catcher is responsible for are those slow tricklers smacked into the ground in front of the plate. And also bunts.

Use both hands anytime you're pursuing a ground ball. Get your mitt down in front of the ball to stop

In fielding the ball in front of the plate, whip off your mask as you dash for the ball. Often you can make the pickup bare-handed.

it, then snatch it up with your bare hand and make the throw. If the play is going to be close, throw sidearm or even underhand.

In obvious bunt situations, take a more erect position behind the plate. Keep your feet closer together. You'll get a faster start when you go for the ball.

Another of the catcher's duties is to back up first base on every throw by an infielder, except, of course, when there are runners on base.

WORKING WITH THE PITCHER—As a catcher, you have to be as much of a student of hitting and hitters as a pitcher. By appraising a batter's grip, stance, and swing, you can sometimes figure out what type of pitch to call for.

Big, strong batters, who usually grip the bat at the very end, like to pull the ball. Curves, low and over the outside corner, are the best pitches to throw to a powerful pull hitter. You can also call for fast balls, letter high to the batter and over the inside corner.

A weaker batter will be bothered by high fast balls. In the case of a batter who stands erect, keep the pitches low in the strike zone.

Study the batter's footwork. For a batter who pulls away from the plate, who "bails out," call for low pitches over the outside corner.

In the case of a batter who stands exceptionally deep in the batter's box, try curves low and outside. For the batter who does the opposite—stands up front in the batter's box—try fast balls inside.

The game situation can also influence the type of pitch you call for. For example, when a sacrifice looms and the batter is intending to bunt, call for pitches that are high and inside. Unless the batter is very careful, he'll hit a pop-up or foul it off.

When there are runners on base and less than two out, keep the ball low and in the strike zone. You're trying to get the batter to hit the ball on the ground, possibly triggering a double play.

Work closely with your pitcher. If he's pitching too fast, slow him down by holding the ball a little longer between pitches, or by delaying the call of the pitch.

Criticize him if you feel the criticism is justified. Encourage him when you feel he needs encouragement.

The best catchers are the ones able to think exactly like their pitchers. They not only know what pitches the man throws and throws best, they also have an understanding of his temperament. They're thus able to coax the best possible performance out of the man at all times.

INFIELD PLAY

You have to have a glove you're happy with in order to be a good fielder. It should fit properly; it should have a pocket that you trust. A good glove helps to make you a confident player.

Figure on paying $25 to $50 for your glove. The higher the grade of leather, the more the glove costs. A better grade of leather means the glove will be more flexible and last longer.

Another sign of quality is the amount of handwork a glove has. The more lacing, for example, the more care went into the glove's manufacture.

Most of the gloves sold in the United States are manufactured in South Korea or Taiwan, even though they carry the names of such American companies as Rawlings, Wilson, Spalding, and Reach. Some of these companies also make gloves in the United States. American-made gloves tend to be manufactured of slightly better leather than those that come from the Orient.

Follow the methods professionals use in breaking in a glove. Pour up to an ounce of water into the glove's pocket, rub it in, then have someone throw hard to you. This "sets" the pocket. Or you can put a baseball in the wetted pocket, wrap the glove tightly with string, and let the glove dry slowly.

Never dry a glove in the sun or in an oven. Doing so cracks the leather.

Once the pocket is set, rub the glove with a drop or two of castor oil. Be careful about using too much oil, which can make the glove heavy and even cumbersome.

Inside the glove, where sweat from your hand can crack the leather, pro players often use a preparation called Lexol to keep the leather soft.

YOUR STANCE—You trot out to your position in the infield, whip the ball around, yell some words of encouragement to your pitcher, and then get set for the first batter. But where do you take your stance? It's not an easy question to answer. It depends on the inning, the score, and who the batter is—whether he's a right-handed or left-handed swinger, a slugger or a slap hitter, and whether he's a fast man on the base paths.

Naturally, for a left-handed hitter you'll play somewhat more toward the right field side of the infield than normal, and for righties you'll move more in the other direction. But there's more to adjusting than this. During batting practice, watch the opposition batters and try to get some indication of the hitting characteristics of each. Who likes to pull the ball? Who likes to go up the middle with it? Who hits fly balls? Who hits grounders?

You also have to be aware of the game situation when you're setting yourself in the infield. With men on base in scoring position, you might play a little deeper than usual. If the batter smashes a hard line drive, you can knock it down and, while you might not throw anyone out, at least you can keep a run from scoring.

There may be other times when your coach instructs you and the other infielders to play "in," in an effort to cut a run off. This means that you play ten to fifteen feet closer to home plate. Sometimes it upsets the batter to see everyone standing on top of him, and he tries too hard and pops up. Other times the strategy backfires; a .180 hitter may bloop the ball over the infield.

Crouch slightly as the pitcher gets set to deliver the ball, your weight distributed evenly on both feet.

Charge any grounder hit to you. Get down low when you make the play. Use an overhand throw in gunning the ball to first base.

In a double play situation with a right-handed hitter at the plate, the shortstop positions himself a few steps closer to the plate. The second baseman comes in, too, but not quite as far. This adjustment assures that either of the two men will be able to get over and cover second base should the ball be hit back to the pitcher.

How you stand is just as important as where you

stand. Get comfortable. Crouch slightly, your arms resting on your thighs or hanging down in front of you. As the pitcher releases the ball, rock forward onto the balls of your feet, leaning in toward the batter. You're alert, ready to move in any direction.

FIELDING THE BALL—When the batter swings and drives the ball in your direction, go for it. What you must never do is back up (unless it's a pop fly over your head) or even lean back. You'll be off-balance. You won't be able to bend over or throw properly. You must be aggressive, always moving toward the ball.

If the ball is slow-hit, really charge. Get your glove down low and let the ball run into it. Occasionally you'll be able to pick up the ball bare-handed.

When the ball is hit hard, also come in on it, even if it's only a step or two. Keep your body low, the knees well bent. Don't take your eyes off the ball. Spread your feet as you glove it, keeping the right foot a bit deeper than the left.

Getting in front of the ball is always a must. Then if it takes a bad hop or you mishandle it, your body will stop it from going through.

Being in front of the ball also means that you'll be able to watch it right up until the instant it enters your glove, which reduces the chance of a misplay.

The glove should be touching the ground. The bare hand is close by, ready to assist. Once the ball arrives, the bare hand reaches in and plucks the ball out.

In the case of a ball that comes bouncing toward you and hops to about the level of your belt, stand more erect. Face the glove toward the ball, the back of your hand facing the ground. Use your bare hand to help guide the ball into the pocket.

When the ball bounces chest high or higher, the back of the glove should be facing your chest. Position the bare hand below the glove pocket. If the ball rebounds out of the glove, the bare hand can snare it.

More often than not, the ball is going to be hit to one side or the other of your body, and you're going to have to dart to your right or left to get it. Cut diagonally whenever you can. If you can't cut diagonally, cut straight across. Just don't go back.

40

In fielding a ball to your left (or right) . . .

Whether you're going to your right or left, your first step should be a crossover step. This means that when you're going to your right, it's left foot over the right foot as the first step. In going left, it's right foot over left. Crossing over gets you away fast.

When you're streaking to your left to field the ball on the run, brake yourself with your left foot. Throw off the right foot.

When you're running to your right, brake with

... **use a crossover step.**

your right foot. Pivot on the right foot, then step toward first base with your left foot as you throw.

When the ball is hit to your right and hit hard, and there's no chance to get in front of it, you'll have to backhand the ball, reaching across your body with your gloved hand. As you reach, step with your left foot; it's a crossover step.

MAKING THE THROW—When you throw, keep the ball about letter high. Use an overhand motion, snapping your wrist as the ball is released. Take only one step. Be sure to follow through. Even if you're smaller than average, the snap throw will enable you to get the ball to its target in a hurry.

When you must throw quickly, try a sidearm delivery. Sidearming is only for short throws, however. It's not likely you can throw sidearm over a long distance and be accurate.

When you have to dash toward the plate to field a slow roller and you have to strain to make the play at first, you might be able to get the ball away successfully with an underhand motion. Be sure you have your eyes on the target as you release. The underhand throw is difficult to catch. Use it only in emergency situations.

CATCHING POP FLIES—Most infielders can handle ground balls with ease, but high pop flies are another matter. Sometimes there's a traffic problem. This is an easy-to-solve problem if you keep a couple of rules in mind and always remember to shout out, "I've got it!" as you go for the ball.

As a general rule, the player coming in on the ball is the one who should make the catch. Thus, pop flies between the catcher and an infielder should be caught by the infielder. The catcher directs traffic on such plays. If the ball is close to home plate and he can get a better angle on the ball than any of the infielders, the catcher makes the play himself.

A pop fly dropping down between infielders and outfielders should be taken by one of the outfielders. As the outfielder comes pounding in, the infielder

On pop flies, get under the ball. Reach up with both hands.

should yell out "Take it! Take it!" Or he might simply shout out the player's name—"Tim! Tim!"

What the infielder shouldn't shout out is "You've got it!" The outfielder might not hear "You've." A base hit—or worse—would be the result.

On short pops, an infielder makes the catch, usually pedaling back, calling for the ball as he goes.

In making the catch, get directly under the ball. You should have the feeling that the ball is going to plummet down on the top of your head. At the last moment, take a step back, reach up with both hands and make the catch.

It takes practice to be able to judge high pops accurately. The mistake most young players make is trying to get lined up from a position that's too far behind the ball. The result is that the ball drops down in front of them. Get *under* the ball as it's coming down.

A sun-filled day can add to your difficulty. Sunglasses can help. Be sure they're the nonbreakable type. Practice with the glasses before you try them in a game.

MAKING THE TAG—Suppose you're covering a base and a runner is tearing toward you. The ball arrives before he does. How do you handle the situation? The first thing to do is straddle the base. Then put your glove in front of it, the ball in the glove pocket.

Just hold the glove there. Don't try to stab at the runner with it. Wait for him to slide, then reach and

When you're covering a base, let the runner slide into the ball and your glove.

tag him. In other words, get the runner to commit himself, then react. What you should avoid doing is committing yourself first with a wild swipe. That enables the runner to elude your tag attempt with his slide.

RUNDOWNS—Whenever infielders have an enemy player in a rundown, it should be a sure out. But frequently the man escapes. It's because mistakes are made.

When you're involved as one of the infielders in a rundown situation, make as few throws as possible. Run the man back toward the base he left. If there's a misplay by one of the fielders and you fail to put the runner out, at least he hasn't advanced.

When you're pursuing the man, keep the ball cocked to throw. This not only enables you to get the ball away quickly, but you can also fake a throw. You can't fake if you're holding the ball at your waist.

Always stay a step or so to the right of the runner. If you don't, he may block your view of the man you're supposed to be throwing to. Also, staying to the right makes it less likely that his body will block a throw.

When you lunge at the runner to make the tag, aim for a target below the level of his belt. He can fake with his arms or his chest and elude you, but it's difficult for him to feint with the lower half of his body.

Each rundown situation demands that the infielders take up different responsibilities. For example, on a rundown between first and second base, the first baseman and the second are usually involved in the rundown in the early stages. The shortstop comes over to cover second base. The pitcher covers first base. In the frenzy of play, these roles may suddenly become reversed. Be sure you know the rundown responsibilities that go with your position.

CUTOFFS—On balls hit to the outfield for one or more bases, one of the infielders frequently acts as a cutoff man, going out into the outfield to take the outfielder's throw and relay it to the catcher in an attempt to nail the runner at the plate. Other times the throw might go to another infielder to prevent the lead runner from advancing.

A typical cutoff play, one involving the third baseman, occurs on a long single to left field with runners on first and second. The third baseman dashes out to shallow left field to take the outfielder's throw and relay the ball to the catcher, the idea being to cut down the runner speeding toward home from second base or at least hold him at third.

You should know the precise role you're going to play as a relay man *before* the play unfolds. If, as in the situation above, you're the third baseman, you should know in advance who's going to be covering third base when you go out to take the throw. (The shortstop is the man most likely to cover.)

You should also know how deep you're going to

go out. This depends on the strength of the outfielder's arm and your arm. If you have the stronger arm, let the outfielder make the shorter throw.

When you're awaiting the outfielder's throw, thrust both hands high in the air, giving the outfielder as big a target as possible. And keep your left foot more toward home plate than your right. This enables you to pivot quickly off your right foot as you turn and drill the ball toward the plate.

You'll get assistance from the catcher or one of the other infielders. For instance, in the situation above, if there's no play at the plate, but a chance to get the runner at third, the catcher will shout "Cut third! Cut third!" You then know that's where you should fire the ball.

PLAYING FIRST BASE

Most first basemen are tall and left-handed. Being tall means that he offers the infielders a king-sized throwing target. Being left-handed makes it much less likely that the runner will obstruct his throws or balls he gets set to catch.

One of the chief responsibilities of the first baseman is to take the throws from the other infielders and make the putout. You, as the first baseman, should sprint into position in front of the base and face the teammate who is fielding the ball and throwing. If the throw is directly toward you, step forward with your left foot, stretch out your glove as far as you can and make the catch. As the ball plunks into your glove, the toe of your right foot should be just touching the bag. (This applies to right-handers. If you're a leftie, step forward with your right foot and touch the base with your left toe.)

On throws that come to you more from the right side, reverse the positioning of your feet—step with your right foot and touch the base with your left toe.

If the infielder uncorks a wild throw and it's out of your reach, get off the bag in a hurry and make the catch. Maybe you can get back to the base in time to make the out, or, in cases where the throw is toward the home plate side of the base, you might be able to tag the runner.

Holding a man on base is another of the first

When receiving a throw from an infielder, stretch as far as you can.

baseman's responsibilities. Take your stance on the home plate side of the base. Your left foot should be near the foul line, and your right foot just touching the corner of the base nearest the pitcher. Crouch slightly, your weight forward on the balls of your feet. Hold the glove outstreched in front of your body, offering a target to the pitcher.

When the pitcher throws over to you and you make the catch, simply drop the glove down in front of the base and let the runner tag himself out. What you shouldn't do is stab at the runner with your glove. He'll simply dodge the tag.

When there is a runner on first and less than two out, you have to be alert for a bunt. If there is a runner on first only, you have to keep him close to the base (by keeping close to it yourself). But as soon as the pitcher releases, rush toward the plate.

When there are runners on first and second, the situation changes. Then you can play in.

On some bunt plays, or slow tricklers you have to rush in to field, the pitcher covers first. Toss the ball to him with an underhanded motion, leading him with the throw so that he can make the catch just as he's crossing the bag. You must practice this play with each of your team's pitchers.

Of course, whenever there's a runner on first, look for a possible double play. On a hard-hit grounder, make the throw to second to get the force play, then sprint to first base for the return throw that will hopefully retire the batter.

Take your stance on the home plate side of first when holding a runner on.

PLAYING SECOND BASE AND SHORTSTOP

As a second baseman, you need to know how to field batted balls cleanly and make quick throws. You have to be able to cover first on bunts and serve as a pivot man on the double play.

The shortstop position is a bit more demanding. Not only must the shortstop accept more fielding chances (since most batters are right-handed), he has more territory to cover than the other infielders. And the throws he must make to first base from deep short are the longest of any infield throws.

A second baseman (and a third baseman) must be able to hit as well as field. The shortstop must be a good fielder. If he's able to hit as well, it's a bonus.

On relays and cutoffs, attempted steals, rundowns, and double plays, the second baseman and shortstop must work together closely. They spend more time practicing together than any other duo.

One of the first things they must establish is who is going to cover second on steal attempts. It's the second baseman who normally covers when a right-handed batter is at the plate, the shortstop in the case of a left-handed batter.

And it's the second baseman who's the relay man when the ball goes into right field. But when the ball goes into left or left center field, he covers sec-

ond base and directs the cutoff throw.

The shortstop is the relay man on hits to left field and left center. He directs the relay and covers second on hits to right field.

Let's examine how the two men work together on a double play. Whether you're performing as the second baseman or shortstop, always be sure to get the first out. There's almost nothing as bad as being so eager that you slip up in making the first out and then the runner streaking for first base beats your throw. You wind up looking for a hole to crawl into.

Another common fault is trying to get the ball to the pivot man before having it under complete control. Keep cool; don't rush.

If you're only a step or two from the bag when

The step-back pivot: As he gets the ball from the short-stop, the second baseman touches the base, then pulls his foot back, and fires to first base.

Here the shortstop is the pivot man; he gets the ball from the second baseman.

you field the ball, step on the base yourself, then make the throw to first. There's no need to involve a teammate as a pivot man.

When you're several feet from the base, feed the ball to the pivot man with a soft underhand toss. Keep it about chin high. This enables the pivot man to get the ball into throwing position with little effort.

If you're more than ten feet or so from the base when you glove the ball, use a snap throw. It's simply a quick, wristy toss.

If you're a second baseman serving as a pivot man, use what's called the "step-back pivot." As you catch the shortstop's toss, touch the bag with your left foot, then draw it back. Last, pushing off of your right foot, make the throw to first.

50

The shortstop touches the base and steps to the outside, then sets up and throws.

As the shortstop, do it this way: As you make the catch, cross the bag to the outside. Then step toward first and make the throw.

As the third baseman, you have to be able to handle line drives.

PLAYING THIRD BASE

While the second baseman and shortstop get more fielding chances and have to develop the precision teamwork necessary to execute double plays, the third baseman has to be able to cope with a greater variety of balls. These range from soft bunts and scratch hits to sizzling line drives. You can't expect to play third base unless you're a superior glove man and have a good arm.

It's usually the third baseman who makes the play on grounds balls hit to his left, which often means he must cut in front of the shortstop. That's OK. It's the third baseman who has the shorter throw, and thus has a better chance of nailing the runner.

On pop flies that sail into foul territory behind third base, it's often the shortstop who makes the play. Since he's positioned deeper, the shortstop is in a better position to get a line on the ball.

Once in a while the third baseman gets a chance to start a double play. When there's a runner on first, you go for the double play by way of second, firing to the pivot man.

The double play that can result when runners are on first and second is easier. After you've fielded the ball, you merely step on third base for the force out, then throw to first to get the batter.

Then there's the double play that can occur when the bases are loaded. After fielding the ball, throw home. The catcher tags the plate for the force, then throws to first.

PLAYING THE OUTFIELD

As the last line of defense, outfielders have to have the ability to be sure-handed in dealing with everything that's hit their way—ground balls, steaming line drives, and towering flies. They have to be able to throw accurately over long distances. They have to have the speed to be able to go and get anything hit toward them.

The center fielder has to have all of these talents in abundance. Since he has more ground to cover than the other two outfielders, he has to be particularly fast. Because he's responsible for more fly balls than the others, he has to be a superior glove man. And throws from deep center demand that he have an exceptionally strong arm.

This is also true of the right fielder. When there's a runner on first base and the batter drills the ball into right field, the right fielder has to be able to rifle the ball all the way to third base (or to a cutoff man who will relay the ball to third), and this is another of the longest of all outfield throws.

Moving for the Ball—Watch a skilled outfielder at work, and he may give you the feeling that he knows in advance where the ball is going to go. Whenever a fly ball is hit anywhere near him, he gets camped under it, ready to make the catch as the ball starts coming down. He never fails to cut off line drives, holding the hitter to one base.

Getting the jump on the ball is what enables him to do these things. By carefully studying each batter and keeping aware of the game situation, he is able to judge where the ball is going to go, and then he simply adjusts his position in the outfield accordingly.

If you're going to play an outfield position, learn to analyze each batter as he comes to the plate and make an effort to determine in advance where the ball is going to go when he hits it. When a left-handed batter comes to the plate, the left fielder automatically comes in a few steps, and the other outfielders move in the direction of the right field foul line. The opposite happens when a right-hander comes to the plate. Everyone moves a few steps toward the left field line, and the right fielder moves in.

Study each batter carefully. If a batter is not particularly strong and chokes up on the bat, you can judge he's not going to rattle the fences. The same is true of the batter who crowds the plate. Move in a few steps.

The batting order itself is another tip-off as to the strengths and weaknesses of the opposition hitters. The lead-off man is likely to be a pesky hitter, capable of slapping out base hits, but he won't be much of a power man. The opposition's power is likely to be found in the third, fourth, and fifth slots of the batting order. Weak hitters are found near the tail end of the lineup.

Always keep track of the ball and strike count. When the batter is ahead in the count (when it's 3 balls, 1 strike, or 2 balls, no strikes), the batter is likely to be swinging freely, trying to lash out an extra-base hit. Be wary. Move deeper by a few steps.

But when the pitcher has the edge (the count is 1 ball, 2 strikes, or 2 balls, 2 strikes), the batter is almost certain to be only trying to meet the ball, get a piece of it. As an outfielder, you can move in a few steps.

Also keep track of the inning, the number of outs, and the score. When a team is trailing by only a run or two in the late innings of a game, the batters behave much differently than if the team had a big lead. Instead of being loose and swinging away, the batters will be playing for one run. They'll be looking for bases on balls and trying to place base hits. You'll see sacrifice bunting and careful base running.

There are other factors that can influence your position in the outfield. The wind, for example. If the wind is blowing toward you, fly balls are going to travel much farther. When the wind is at your back, fly balls are going to go higher and stay up in the air longer. Winds blowing to the right or left affect the ball accordingly. Check flags or chimney smoke to determine the wind's direction. Or toss a few tufts of grass into the air and watch in which direction they blow.

If the sun becomes a problem, wear sunglasses or shield your eyes with your glove.

STANCE—You'll also help yourself get a jump on the ball by using the right stance. Spread your feet at least shoulder-width apart and crouch slightly. Keep your weight evenly concentrated on both feet.

Your hands should hang loosely in front of your body, or keep them on your knees.

As the pitcher goes into his windup, concentrate on the batter. Rock forward slightly onto the balls of your feet. Now you're ready to move in any direction.

If the batter doesn't go for the ball, or swings and misses, you can straighten up and relax. But when the pitcher steps on the rubber and gets set to throw, assume your ready position again.

When you go for the ball, always use a crossover step. If the ball is hit to your right, take your first step with your left foot. In the case of a ball hit to your left, your first step should be with your right foot. (The crossover step is pictured in the section of this book titled "Infield Play.")

When the ball is hit over your head, don't back-pedal. Turn and run back, keeping your eyes on the ball by looking over your shoulder as you run.

When you move for the ball, always run on the balls of your feet. Don't run with flat-footed strides. Running on the balls of your feet enables you to run fast and glide.

HANDLING GROUNDERS—If there's no one on base when a ground ball comes your way, drop down on one knee when you make the play. This enables you to block the ball and still get it back to the infield in a hurry.

When men are on base, it's a different story. You must sprint toward the ball, get in front of it, and

When a grounder comes your way, charge the ball. Get in front of it in making the play.

play it just as an infielder would.

Be relaxed when you're fielding ground balls. Don't stab at the ball with your glove. Handle it with "soft" hands.

Young players often make more misplays on grounders than on fly balls. If you have problems in this department, do some practicing with your team's infielders.

FLY BALLS—Always use two hands to make the catch when catching a fly ball. Don't let yourself be influenced by those major league outfielders who use a one-handed style. In the 1979 World Series, Dave Parker of the Pirates, a true superstar, dropped a fly ball when attempting to make a one-handed catch. Two hands are always better than one.

From the instant the ball leaves the bat, follow it with your eyes. Concentrate on it until it plunks into your glove. This tip will help you to judge exactly where the ball is going to come down. If you don't learn to keep your eyes glued on the ball, you won't make nearly as many catches as you should.

On any high fly, make the catch at about the level of your head. Then if you should bobble the ball, you still have a chance to recover the ball before it hits the ground.

In the case of a low line drive, position your glove with the palm facing up. Make the catch with a scooping motion.

Beware of shoestring catches, those you try to make at your shoe tops. In attempting a shoestring catch, you can easily turn a potential single into an extra-base hit. It's almost always wiser to play the ball on one bounce.

COMMUNICATING—It's vital that the outfielders communicate with one another. When you and another outfielder are going for the ball, and you feel you are in a better position to make the catch, shout out "I've got it! I've got it!" But if you think your teammate has a better line on the ball, yell "Take it! Take it!"

Always use both hands when gloving a fly ball.

56

Outfielders should also help out one another when a fence presents a hazard. Suppose your teammate drifts back to make a catch near a fence. Either advise him "Plenty of room!" or warn him that a collision looms.

Also direct the other outfielders as to where to throw the ball. While your teammate is setting up to make a catch or field the ball, you should keep track of what's happening on the basepaths. "Third base!" you can tell him as he makes the catch. Then he won't have to delay an instant in getting the ball away.

THROWING—Holding the ball, even for a split second, is one of the most serious mistakes an outfielder can make. Whether you're fielding a ground ball or catching a fly, you should know in advance what you're going to do with the ball once you have it in your possession. Get it to the right base or cutoff man immediately.

When catching a fly ball, keep your left foot slightly ahead of your right. This will help you to get the ball away quickly. Be certain to follow this advice in any tag-up situation.

As this may imply, take only one step when you make your throw. For every extra step you take, the runner is advancing a step.

Use an overhand delivery when you throw. This puts backspin on the ball, which helps to make the throw accurate. Don't throw with a sidearm motion. Sidearming causes the ball to curve or hook.

Whenever possible, outfielders should back up one another.

Keep the throw low so it can be cut off. Unless the throw is a short one, make it on one hop. A low, hard throw that bounces once gets to the target much faster than a sky-high, no-bounce throw.

If you're throwing to a relay man, aim for his head. When the ball arrives head high, he'll be able to make the catch and throw in one motion.

Always be ready to back up your teammates. If you're the left fielder, for instance, angle behind the center fielder on ground balls hit to him, ready to make the play should the ball go through him. Also go back to assist him on deep fly balls, particularly those that might carom off the fence.

Outfielders should also back up the infielders. The left fielder backs up second base on throws that come from the opposite side of the diamond. He also backs up third base on bunts and pick-offs. The right fielder does the same on the other side of the field. The centerfielder backs up plays at second base.

As all of this suggests, there's much more to playing the outfield than catching flies and fielding grounders. You have to stay alert every second. If you're not watchful and in control, you're going to be surprised. And every time you get surprised, you're likely to make a mistake.

DEFENSIVE PLAY

Baseball, being a team game, requires that the nine players on the field work together like a well-oiled machine. Every time the batter smacks the ball, the entire team swings into action. Every player has a job to do.

① Pitcher	⑦ Left Fielder
② Catcher	⑧ Center Fielder
③ First Baseman	⑨ Right Fielder
④ Second Baseman	Ⓧ Base Runner
⑤ Third Baseman	o o o Batted Ball
⑥ Shortstop	- - - - Thrown Ball

Key to diagrams

The diagrams in this chapter depict players' responsibilities in typical defensive situations. Study the role you should play in each case. You should train yourself to react automatically to whatever happens on the field. Even a moment's hesitation can be costly.

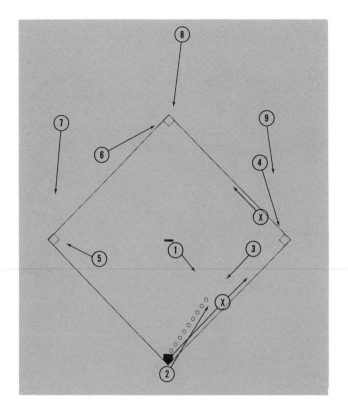

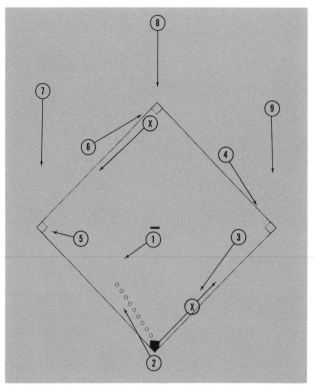

Sacrifice Bunt, Runner on First Base—This situation occurs frequently. The bunt has been struck toward first base. Both the catcher (2) and the first baseman (3) dart forward in an attempt to field the ball, with the catcher sizing up the situation and shouting instructions. Note how the other fielders move to cover the bases. The outfielders come in to back up the infielders.

Sacrifice Bunt, Runner on Second Base—Either the pitcher (1) or the catcher (2) makes the fielding play in this situation, with the third baseman (5) hurrying back to cover the base. Had the bunt been laid down on the other side of the diamond, play would be similar, with the first baseman taking the throw from either the pitcher or the catcher.

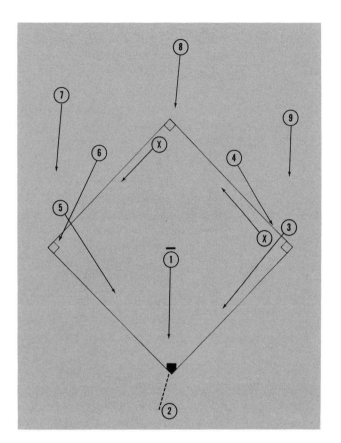 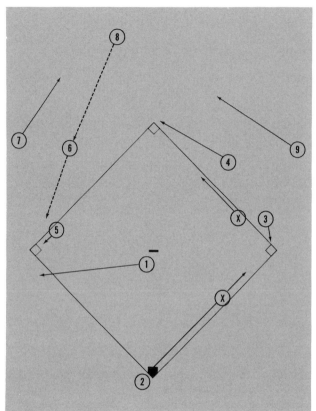

WILD PITCH, RUNNERS ON FIRST AND THIRD—
As the catcher (2) races back to retrieve the ball,
the pitcher (1) darts in to cover home plate. As the
catcher picks up the ball, the pitcher shouts out
instructions, telling him whether he should hold the
ball or throw it, and, if he is to throw, to which base.

SINGLE TO CENTER FIELD, RUNNER ON FIRST—
The center fielder (8) and the shortstop (6), serving as the cutoff man, work together in this situation
to prevent the runner on first base from advancing
beyond second. The pitcher (1) backs up at third
base.

60

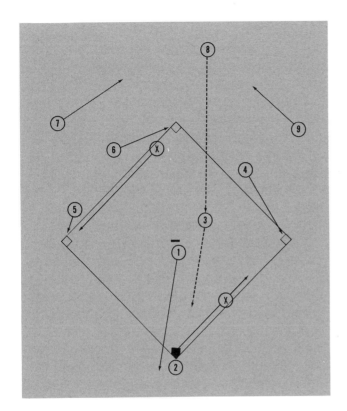

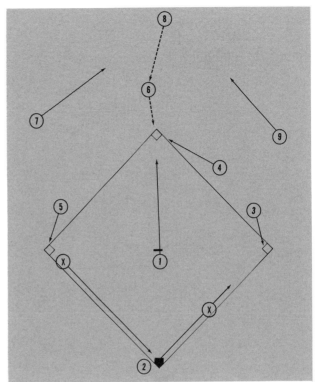

SINGLE TO CENTER FIELD, RUNNER ON SECOND BASE—The idea here is to get the ball to the catcher (2) as quickly as possible to prevent the run from scoring. The center fielder (8) fires to the first baseman (3), who relays the ball to the catcher. If the ball is hit very deep and there's no chance to prevent the run from scoring, the throw goes to the shortstop (6), who's covering second.

SINGLE TO CENTER FIELD, RUNNER ON THIRD BASE—When there's a runner on third base and the ball goes rocketing into the outfield, there can be no play on the runner; he lopes home with ease. It's the outfielder's responsibility to get the ball to second base, holding the hitter at first. In the situation depicted here, the center fielder (8) makes use of the shortstop (6), who's acting as the cutoff man.

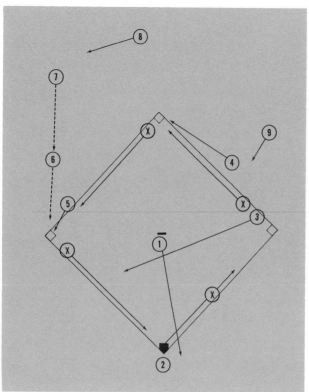

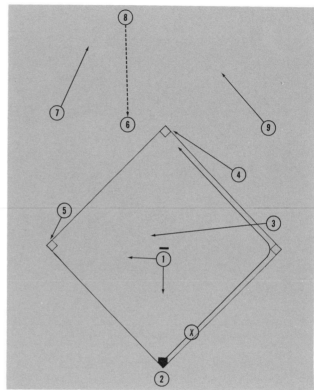

SINGLE TO LEFT FIELD, BASES LOADED—The left fielder (7) is most likely to throw to the shortstop (6) in this situation. The shortstop, in turn, relays the ball to third base, where the third baseman (5) is covering. But the left fielder can also try for a play at the plate, in which case he'll use the first baseman (3) as his relay man. The pitcher (1) backs up the catcher.

EXTRA BASE HIT, BASES EMPTY—On this long drive to center field, the shortstop (6) is the relay man. Once he gets the ball in his possession, the shortstop throws to either the third baseman (5) or the catcher (2), depending on where the base runner happens to be. The first baseman (3) slants over to the middle of the diamond; his job is to cut off the relay if he feels *he* has a play.

GLOSSARY

BALK—An illegal movement by the pitcher that might deceive the base runner.

BAIL OUT—To step away from the plate to avoid being hit by a pitched ball.

BATTER'S BOX—The 6' by 4' lined-off area on either side of home plate within which the batter must stay when hitting.

CHANGE, CHANGE-UP, CHANGE OF PACE—A slow pitch thrown for deception with the same motion as a fast ball.

COUNT—The number of balls and strikes on the batter.

CUTOFF—Interception of a throw, usually from an outfielder, by an infielder other than the one for whom the throw is intended.

DRAG BUNT—A bunt made for a base hit (rather than sacrificing), usually by a left-handed batter, who attempts to "drag" the ball down the first base line.

FORCE PLAY—A situation in which a base runner must attempt to reach the next base. On a force play, the fielder has only to touch the base for the runner to be out.

HIT AND RUN—A play in which the runner on first base breaks for second base on the pitch. The batter then tries to hit the pitch toward the position vacated by the infielder.

JAM—To throw a pitch close to a hitter's hands, preventing him from taking a full swing.

JUMP—On an attempted steal, the advantage the base runner gains over the pitcher by virtue of his lead and getaway move.

PICK-OFF—To catch a runner off base for a putout.

PIVOT MAN—The fielder who makes the first putout on a double play attempt.

POP FLY—A high fly ball within or just beyond the infield.

PULL HITTER—A right-handed batter who hits to left field, and a left-handed batter who hits to right field.

PUTOUT—The act of putting a player out.

RBI—See Run batted in.

RELAY—A throw from an infielder, who has just taken a throw from an outfielder, to a third teammate.

RUBBER—The rectangular slab of white rubber that measures 6 by 24 inches and which is set in the pitcher's mound. The pitcher must remain in contact with the rubber during the pitch.

RUN BATTED IN—A run that scores as a direct result of offensive action (a base hit, base on balls, sacrifice fly, etc.) by the batter.

RUNDOWN—A situation in which a base runner is caught between bases and forced to run in one direction and then the other between opposing players while they toss the ball back and forth in attempting to make the tag.

SACRIFICE BUNT—A bunt made with less than two out which advances the base runner and on which the batter is put out.

SACRIFICE FLY—A fair or foul ball hit with less than two out that is caught for an out and that is long enough to allow a base runner to tag up and score.

WILD PITCH—A pitch thrown past the catcher that permits a base runner to advance.